The Itsy Bitsy Spider

pictures by

MEREDITH JOHNSON

McGraw Hill **Wright Group**

www.WrightGroup.com

 **Wright Group**

Send all inquiries to:
Wright Group/McGraw-Hill
P.O. Box 812960
Chicago, IL 60681

ISBN 0-07-572895-8

7 8 9 QST 09 08 07 06

The itsy bitsy spider
went up the water spout.

Down came the rain

and washed the spider out.

Out came the sun

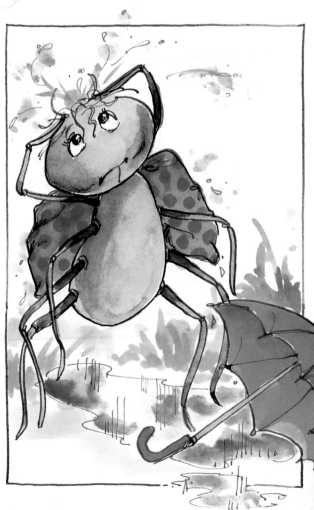

and dried up all the rain,

and the itsy bitsy spider

went up the spout again.

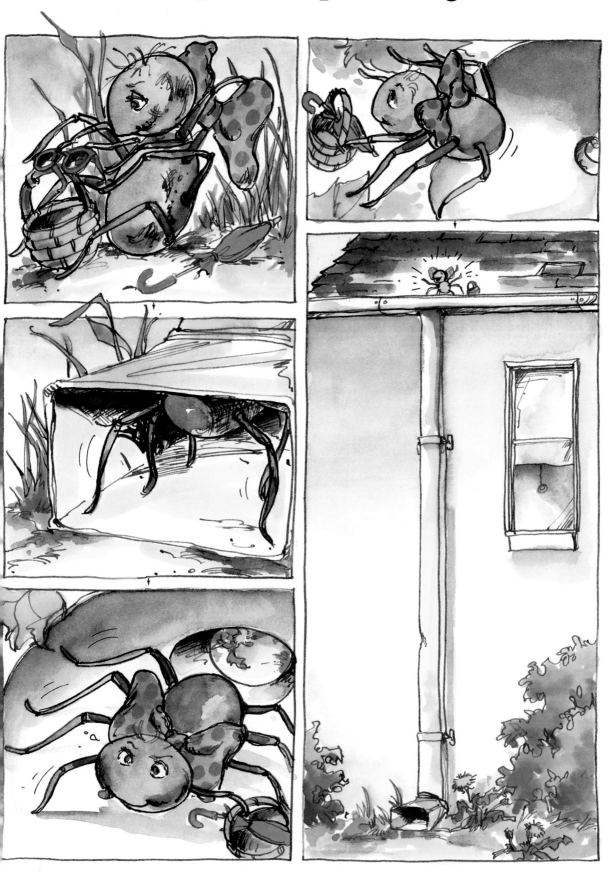

The itsy bitsy spider
went up the water spout.

Down came the rain
and washed the spider out.

Out came the sun
and dried up all the rain,

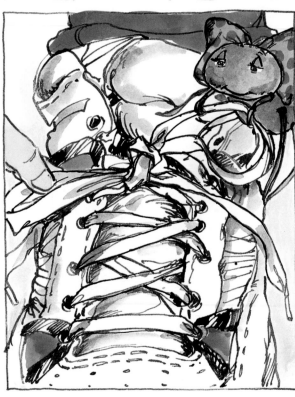

and the itsy bitsy spider
went up the spout again.

The itsy bitsy spider
went up the water spout.

Down came the rain
and washed the spider out.

Out came the sun
and dried up all the rain,

and the itsy bitsy spider...

You know the rest.

The itsy bitsy spider
went up the water spout.

Down came the rain
and washed the spider out.

You know the rest.

The itsy bitsy spider
went up the water spout.

Down came the rain and. . .

Say the rest by yourself.

The itsy bitsy spider
went up the water spout. . . .

Say the rest by yourself.

Say it by yourself.